Sometimes I Dance When I Walk

A COLLECTION OF THOUGHT
1979-1985

BRITT BOSWELL

ROSE PUBLISHING COMPANY
LITTLE ROCK

© 1985 by Britt Boswell

Boswell, Britt.
    Sometimes I dance when I walk.

    I. Title.
PS3552.O812   811.54
ISBN 0-914546-60-0

Library of Congress Catalog Number 85-72098

So how is it that
I left and arrived
at the same time?

Dedicated to
my Family, my Friends.

THOUGHTS/Britt Boswell

". . . all life and art are justified by communication; experiences are to share, not hoard."
       ANSEL ADAMS

The Plow

Old oaken handles
With rusted runners
A timeless tool endures
. . .working with Earth.

    Nov., 1979.

Our Humanity

We have a lot. . .
Though our differences are many
Our similarities are in abundance
. . .we have a lot.

    Jan., 1980.

Being has its changes. . .
Hope to Hopelessness,
(Life to Death).

    Sept., 1982.

THOUGHTS/Britt Boswell

An Experience

With plastic tubes sustaining life.
With smiling faces to make it easier.

The anxious sleep with plastic tubes.
The smiling faces with sharp needles
. . .to make it easier.

Is life just a trip down a hallway?
With smiling faces, plastic tubes and sharp needles
. . .to make it easier.

Is this darkness a finality? no;
An awakening with smiling faces and plastic tubes
. . .to make it easier.

                                        Sept., 1982.

THOUGHTS/Britt Boswell

Strong Stone Fence

The digging, the lifting, the stacking of hard, heavy stone.
The toil of the folk working with the land.
A stone fence now stretches for miles . . . and miles.
From what was once a rock-strewn field,
Now is a green pasture surrounded by a strong, stone fence
. . .a beautiful green pasture, a strong, stone fence.

Oct., 1982.

A Rock, For Sharing

Four folks searched,
Then they found,
The perfect rock to be shared.

It wasn't too large,
And rose to great height;
It figured to reveal quite a lot.

The folks climbed up,
Clung tight to that rock,
Then smiled at the thoughts that they shared.

Oct., 1982.

THOUGHTS/Britt Boswell

An Anesthetic Sleep

Rolling down the hallway with fear in your heart,
. . .that fear with 170 beats a minute.

A beautiful body comes by to tell you to relax,
. . .relax to the tune of 170 beats a minute.

Into the O.R. with fear in your heart,
. . .that's the operating room at 170 beats a minute.

A white mask with smiling eyebrows tells you to relax,
. . .and breathe into a cold, coarse, rubber tube.

About to go under with fear in your heart,
. . .suddenly not giving a damn about 170 beats a minute.

A cold numbness comes before the darkness,
. . .the darkness called the anesthetic sleep.

That mysterious sleep where you awaken only with your ears,
. . .while your eyes just keep rolling and closing.

No dreams, no recollections, just noise and confusion,
. . .who are these white masks with smiling eyebrows?

An anesthetic sleep is only a noisy and confused awakening.

                                              Oct., 1982.

THOUGHTS/Britt Boswell

The River

Brown Water Runnin'
Runnin' Hard With White
Brown, Shakin' Trees
Logs Rollin' With White
Runnin', Shakin', Rollin'
. . .Eternal Power!

        Oct., 1982.

Old Wealth

Wasted amid the island dunes,
Carnegie money done in by time.
Time full of winds, rains and growth.
Growth of palms, shrub, grass and vine.
Vine that clings to the remains of old wealth.

        Oct., 1982.

Old Wealth

THOUGHTS/Britt Boswell

The Trail

Rounding the bend
. . .a sudden downpour,
Dampness to the bone,
Sign: Keep On The Trail.

Rounding the bend
. . .a not-so-sudden downpour,
Dampness to the marrow,
Sign: Keep On The Trail.

Rounding the bend
. . .the all-too-familiar downpour,
Dampness is a relative thing,
Sign: Scenic Waterfall 500 Feet.

Good thing we 'kept' on the trail.

Oct., 1982.

THOUGHTS/Britt Boswell

In Living Color

Light Strokes of Brilliance
Right Before Our Eyes
    In Living Color
The Autumn Canvas Awash!

                Oct., 1982.

A Wind Of Change

A wind of change, cool change,
Sweeps in with the bright September skies.
A wind of colors, the Fall colors,
On the trees right before my eyes.

It's a nice wind, the Autumn wind,
A wind of colors, a wind of change.

                Oct., 1982.

THOUGHTS/Britt Boswell

A Pool, In The Fall

Caught between the Summer's stagnation
And the Winter's pristine magic,
A pool, in the Fall,
Takes on a somewhat murky clarity.

While it is clearing just enough
To detect the lively movements within,
It remains murky, just enough,
To prevent the detection of the movers.

This pool of murky clarity serves
As a collector of Autumn's fallen colors,
The leaves, lifting from the trees,
And lightly floating through the air.

Into the pool of murky clarity,
Floating here, sinking there,
The aimless float, with each new breeze,
Serving to brighten the murky clarity. . .

That is a pool, in the Fall.

                                            Oct., 1982.

THOUGHTS/Britt Boswell

". . . some scarce see Nature at all. But to the eyes of the 'man' of imagination, Nature is imagination itself. As a 'man' is, so he sees."

William Blake.

The Barn

Old, Aged Wood,
Splittin' Dark Gray.
Rough, Rusted Roof,
Washed With Rain.
Built With The Earth
. . .To Stay.

        Oct., 1982.

The Mountains Appalachian

Mountains, surrounded by mountains.
Mist, lingering through the valleys.
Streams, trickle, then rush through rock and pine.
Time, standing still for mountain, mist and stream.

Folk, touched by the mountains appalachian.

        Oct., 1982.

THOUGHTS/Britt Boswell

Purple At The Summit

Rising into the dense, gray cloud,
A mountain among mountains,
Its peak lost in the dark mist.
A trail winds its way to the top,
At once flat and forested,
Then steep and barren.
Above the tree line now, amidst the gray.
Low, brown grasses whisper in the wind.
There, tucked beneath a solitary spruce,
Flowers . . . purple at the summit.

                            Oct., 1982.

Canyon Of Grandness

Seen only from the edge
With colors of brilliance
Stroked with fingers of light
This canyon of grandness
Moved us with the colors
Stroked us with the light.

                 Oct., 1982.

THOUGHTS/Britt Boswell

Sea Oats Bending

Living there in a sea of white,
Under blue sky, tall, brown sea oats, bending.

Sea of white, rolling near the coastal waters,
Sandy hills, turning flat under surf, pounding.

Tall, brown grasses holding white hills steady,
Shaped by the constant sea breeze, blowing.

Living in the sea of white, blown by the constant breeze,
These are the tall, brown sea oats, bending.

                                                Oct., 1982.

A Beautiful Road (The Plantation Dream)

A beautiful road going nowhere
One wonders where it had been
With trees of great height
On each side just right
It must have been from a dream.

Indeed, it was dreamed,
It was not what it seemed!
A beautiful road, (the plantation dream), going nowhere.

                                                Oct., 1982.

Beautiful Road

THOUGHTS/Britt Boswell

The Meetin' Place

It was a simple little meetin' place,
Good place to get folk to gather.
It was "white-washed" and boarded up,
Set back from the dusty, dirty road.
Sunday comes and that road gets dustier,
That simple little meetin' place gets full of folk.

Full of soul, full of hope . . . Amen, Lord have mercy on us all!

Oct., 1982.

A.D. 1982, we shall make sense of this. Hope is a song not yet sung, a path not yet taken, a smile amid the tears, the birth of a child, a new friendship, a whisper among the shouting, a light in the darkness. Hope happens.

Oct., 1982.

THOUGHTS/Britt Boswell

A Tree, Starkly Standing

Through the hard rain,
    then cool mist,
The long climb leads
    to the mountaintop.

Set against a heavy, wet fog,
    it rises tall and bare.

With its half limbs,
    twisted and stumped,
A tree starkly stands,
    defying its deathly appearance.

It remains. . .
    to be seen.

                  Oct., 1982.

Cool Stream Soul

Cool Stream
Fog Shroud
Penetrating Dampness
To The Soul.

        Oct., 1982.

THOUGHTS/Britt Boswell

A Fall Day, Visualized

White ducks swimming across the even surface of a lake,
With red, yellow and blue reflections of tree and sky.
Bright yellow, that is the old elm, spreading in the sunlight,
With the tall pine rising behind that is evergreen.
Gray mockingbird perched upon the low, green shrubbery,
Nervously twitching with the black cat's every move.
The sinking sun filtering through the shimmering leaves
Of the smaller trees, that ends a fall day, visualized.

           Oct. 31, 1982.

A Mainstreet Gone By

Decay, no sign of the Rush that once was.
A dirty road, lined with half-fallen houses.
Big, old trees, hiding the broken business facades.
The city of Rush, a mainstreet gone by.

           Oct., 1982.

THOUGHTS/Britt Boswell

The Spirit Of The Place

*It's a soft serenity that always pervades,
With the tall trees and the lawn, immaculate;
And the moss hanging silently all around.*

*It's an unimposing gentleness that beckons
To that structure of purity, seemingly at One
With the Moss and the Trees and the Lawn.*

*The structure that has stood for a century, ageless.
The structure that embodies the spirit of the place.*

           Oct., 1982.

The Spirit of the Place

THOUGHTS/Britt Boswell

Picasso's Dancers

Hands Clasped, Joyously,
As if in Celebration,
In Celebration of Living,
Of Living and Being,
Being with Others,
Being with Other Hands to Clasp.

Joyously, in Dance;
Joyously, in Celebration;
Joyously, in Living.

                    Oct., 1982.

THOUGHTS/Britt Boswell

My Harmonica

Sitting idle in my desk drawer,
My harmonica waits for me.
It never does anything more,
Knowing one day it will set me free.
I wish my harmonica would just jump out and play,
Though I know it will be some other day.

. . .It's the possibilities in life
    That make it worth living.

                                        Oct., 1982.

Ode To Bobby

Boy meets girl, girl wants another.
Boy meets another girl, girl wants to be alone.
Winter turns to Spring, snow turns to rain.
Wise old redhead said, "Life's Weird."

                                        Oct., 1982.

THOUGHTS/Britt Boswell

Sunset Living

A dark stand of pine
Frame a splash of orange
Painting across the horizon
So glorious that neither pen
Nor brush can capture that moment.

Only heart and soul
Capture the sunset;
With the next day's living
That moment will find expression.
Sunset, for the next day's living.

      Oct., 1982.

Sunset In South Carolina

Hidden just enough by the dark gray clouds,
  the sun revealed itself as a stream of orangeness.

It was just above the distant horizon,
  reflecting peacefully on a salt marsh mirror.

Captured on film, a moment of nature's perfection,
  flawed only by gray lines, running horizontally.

. . .Damn those power lines! Damn those power lines!

      Oct., 1982.

THOUGHTS/Britt Boswell

The Fence, Split Rail

Running back, then forth,
  the fence, split rail
Runs 'round the home place;
  logs split, then stacked
Run 'round the corn rows;
  logs stacked, then crossed
Run 'round the tool shed;
  the fence, split rail,
Legacy to its maker.

                    Oct., 1982.

The Island

Human transportation to desolation, vegetation,
forestation, flea-infestation . . . for a short visitation.

                    Oct., 1982.

THOUGHTS/Britt Boswell

Ritz Crackers (Actually Chicken in a Biscuit)

Red hair, red bandana, red eyes;
  Too much drivin'
Birds, birds and more birds;
  Too many birds.
Ritz crackers on the table;
  Too many Ritz.

Crackers Take Flight
With The Birds
In The Breeze;
. . .Nice Lunch.

Oct., 1982.
Dedicated to Robert "Bob," "Bobby" Lyford (and birds).

THOUGHTS/Britt Boswell

Woodworking Hands

Old, rough, red, skillful hands,
Hands that cut and scrape and scratch.

Old, delicate, red, skillful hands,
Hands that feel and shape and create.

Hands of a lifetime. . .
Of cutting, scraping, scratching.

Hands of experience. . .
Of feeling, shaping, creating.

. . .Woodworking Hands.

      Oct., 1982.

A Lot To Tell

With a wrinkled, graying, unshaven face,
Eyes deep-set, sometimes sad, othertimes twinkling,
Oftentimes with cane and red suspenders,
A man of experience points while talking. . .

Talking of a history, a past, a lifetime.
It had been a "checkered" lifetime . . . indeed.
Talented with his hands, the hands of a cook,
A carpenter, a musician and still a painter.

Still a painter "with good perspective."
Still a painter with a lot to tell.
(and I felt fortunate to be able to listen).

      Oct., 1982.

THOUGHTS/Britt Boswell

Cascading Strands (With Accompaniment by Rhythmic Bongoes)

Cascading Strands
Bathing Folk and Rock,
Smooth, Cool Rock,
Rough, Hot Folk.

Cascading Strands
Doing it right!

    Oct., 1982.

Solitude Pool

Empty Trees,
Cold, Cold Breeze,
By a Solitude Pool,
A Pool of Depth,
Sits a Solitary Figure,
A Figure Deep in Solitude,
By Empty Trees,
In the Cold, Cold Breeze,
... .Solitude Pool.

    Oct., 1982.

THOUGHTS/Britt Boswell

(The Light Shines Brightest By. . .)
Dark, Solitary, Spruce Trees

Basking, on the bright white hillside,
A single, solitary figure and spruce tree
Awashed in the snowy light.

Awaken single solitary figures!
Bask in the bright light by
Dark, solitary, spruce trees,

               Oct., 1982.

Misty Mountain Sea

Cool, dark gray air blowin',
Cool, dark gray water rollin',
Cool, dark gray rock sittin',
Misty Mountain sea livin',
Cool, Dark, Gray.

               Oct., 1982.

THOUGHTS/Britt Boswell

Nice Talkin' To You . . . Again

Well, sure was nice talkin' to you again,
It'd been years, jeepers, at least ten!

It's funny how we slipped out of touch,
More or less just livin' our lives, and such.
Wonder if it'd been different if it'd been five, not ten,
Shoot, you'd still not gone through your divorce then!

What a difference the years make,
Seems like they don't give much, just take. . .

Away more years; nice talkin' to you . . . again.

Oct., 1982.

THOUGHTS/Britt Boswell

Mountain Man

With a wrinkled face and grizzled beard,
A strong back and even stronger mind,
A tired, old man talked of being exposed...
    Exposed to a stingy survival.
    Exposed to all that is nature.
    Exposed to his innermost self.
He said he was ready to Go;
But before he Went,
He spoke these words: Get Exposed!

                            Oct., 1982.

The Most Beautiful Smile

With long, long, lightly brown hair,
Gently framing a face full of warmth,
Warmth radiating from cheek to cheek,
Cheeks surrounding a very peaceful mouth,
A mouth softly speaking, full of wonder,
While revealing wonderfully white teeth,
Wonderfully white teeth smiling a deep smile,
A deep smile, the most beautiful smile.

                            Oct., 1982.

A Memory
    Like that time driving through the Virginia mountains, at dawn, with that folk music on the radio, feeling alive and awake.

THOUGHTS/Britt Boswell

A Party

Walking hurriedly to
    the white house on the left.
Into a crowd of others
    drinking hurriedly in
    the white house on the left.
Another crowd of others, hurriedly drunken,
    hurry through the front door of
    the white house on the left.
The J. Geils Band hurriedly whips
    the others into a frenzy in
    the white house on the left.

Walking hurriedly comes the resident of
    the white house on the left.
The crowd of others hurriedly punch holes, heavily,
    into the ceilings, the walls, the door of
    the white house on the left.
The resident lays down her weary head
    as the crowd of others leaves
    the white house on the left.
Walking hurriedly,
    I search for another
    crowd of others.

                                    Oct., 1982.

THOUGHTS/Britt Boswell

Early Morning, On The Train

It was early morning, on the train;
Enduring a sleepless sleep in a hazy light;
The slow, easy rocking that is the train on rails,
With sudden stops, then not-so-sudden starts.
Sunrise, and everything is shown anew.
Winding in and out, darkness, then light,
Tunnels, with blackness blacker than night.
Mountains, with a sudden steepness, rise outside the berth.
The mountains, rising high, while the misty morning still is low.
Snow-capped, then barren, always in and out of blackness,
The beauty of these mountains enjoyed between tunnels,
In the early morning, on the train.

           Oct., 1982.

Water Way
  Falling Faster, Faster
Rushng, Swirling . . . Angry.
Slowly Stagnating
Still, Silent . . . Tranquil.
Cutting Its Course
A Giver of Life, a Mirror of Life.

     Oct., 1982.

THOUGHTS/Britt Boswell

The Innocent

Small
*   Deep, Dark Eyes;*
Small
*   Cold, Wet Nose;*
Small
*   Shaky, Wandering Legs;*
Trusting, Reaching, Smiling Innocence.

                    Oct., 1982.

Boxes Full Of Letters Kept

Letters,
*   of thoughts and feelings shared;*
Letters Kept,
*   testimonials to share companionships;*
Boxes Full of Letters Kept,
*   all that is left of companionship.*

It sure gets lonely now,
With only boxes full of letters kept.

                    Oct., 1982.

THOUGHTS/Britt Boswell

Habits of Over-extension

Oftentimes long distance,
Never in the morning,
Always for a friend,
These habits of over-extension,
Are certainly hard to break.

                Oct., 1982.

For A Great Appreciation

A sadness, that lasts all day
In a world of diversions and avoidance,
A true sadness that leads to
A greater appreciation of happiness.

Sadness, now much more truly experienced.
Happiness, now much more deeply felt.

                Oct., 1982.

THOUGHTS/Britt Boswell

Two Logs, Fallen
    (A Story)

Two Logs, Fallen;
One Fallen Here,
The Other Fallen There.

Two Folks Walkin';
One Walkin' Here,
The Other Walkin' There.

Swift Stream Flowin';
One Folk Drops One Log Here,
The Other Drops One Log There.

Two Folks Crossin'
The Stream,
Together.

Moral: Better to Cross
       Those Swift Streams
       With Another
       (and two logs).

                        Oct., 1982.

THOUGHTS/Britt Boswell

Peace Day (People Gathered To Celebrate Peace)

People gathered to celebrate Peace.
    Peace is not simply life without war;
    Peace is a way of living.
There are those who believe this way of living
    is achieved through military strength,
    a "Peace Through Strength."
There is another kind of strength,
    the strength to believe in your fellow human being;
    to believe that all of the Creator's children
    have a right to exist;
    to believe that understanding humanity's diversity
    is important to gain Peace.
It takes an inner strength to accept humanity's diversity,
    it is with this strength that true Peace will be achieved.
    A great book says, "Blessed are the Peacemakers;"

Now is the time to gain that inner strength
    necessary to become a Peacemaker
        Oct., 10, 1982.
        . . .a contribution
        to celebration of the first
        Peace Day, 1982

THOUGHTS/Britt Boswell

The Cold That Is The Shadows

The cold, dark and gray, blows in suddenly,
As the distant sunlight strains to cast
The long shadows that come late in the day.

The cold, dark and gray, and the shadows, long and black,
Serve to block the warmth that is the colors of the Fall;
These colors that were so warm, give way now to the cold,

To the cold that is the shadows.

Nov., 1982.

The Tangled Mess

The wildness of these woods,
With tall pines towering
Over the darkened underbrush,
It's a tangled mess,
With the gray trees,
All bark and limb,
And the green vines,
Curled, long and thick,

Wildness, yes, just enough.

Nov., 1982.

THOUGHTS/Britt Boswell

A Fulfilling Moon

A circle of brightness clearly defined
Against the blackness that is the night.
It illuminates branches of tall, leafless trees.
It sets off sounds in the densely wooded countryside.
It brings the still blackness to life.

As you sit under a leafless tree,
You can sense the stirrings of life in the night;
Stirred by a fulfilling moon.

        Nov., 1982.

The Way of Life, Lived
  A steady stream of distance passed.
  The encounters, intimate or otherwise,
  With man, woman, child and nature.
  Stormy, turbulent; then quiet, calm;
  The way of life, lived, inside and out.

        Nov., 1982.

THOUGHTS/Britt Boswell

On Being Photographic In The Wintertime

Put away the Kodacolor,
Bring out the black and white.
The winter is upon us now;
A time of starkness, contrast.

Wait, for the snows, and the ice
On the trees, and the limbs,
With the shadows, and the clouds
Gray, with black and white.

                Nov., 1982.

Escapism

As practiced by those
who leave a crowded
movie theater with their
chin down, eyes to the floor,
and forehead pressed into
the back of another,
each headed in the direction
of the lighted exit sign
seen only when entering
the darkened room.

                Nov., 1982.

THOUGHTS/Britt Boswell

On That Matter Of Time

My friends will all be married soon,
I guess it was only a matter of time.
I'm still sitting alone, again,
Waiting on that matter of time.
I hope she has a beautiful smile,
A smile that's both bright and deep.
She doesn't have to do the cooking,
So long as she stays around to eat.
I hope she's able to share and teach,
Those things that make life really matter.
Most of all, I really just hope
It's only a matter of time.

      Nov., 1982.

That moment of pain, the pull, the tug, wears you down, down, deeper down, searching inside, only to find that is no place to hide, so you just let go, say goodbye, and that moment is no more.

THOUGHTS/Britt Boswell

If Only For A Visit

It was only for a visit,
Unable to even make "a day of it,"
With only a few hours to work with,
Remembering to make "the most of it."

Unfamiliar faces . . . a "smile" and "hello,"
Familiar faces bring back an inner warmth;
Those who mean the most get a firm embrace,
And share in some of that inner warmth.

"Touching base" on matters of importance.
"Sending signals" for future reference.
Remembering how much these moments really matter,
These people really matter.

All in a few hours of "touching base" and "sending signals;"
Just making "the most of it," if only for a visit.

Nov., 1982.

THOUGHTS/Britt Boswell

My Life, Put To Music

I'm gonna put my life to music,
'Cause I've got the blues. . .
My life's in the gutter
And besides, my guitar's out of tune.

> Nov. 15, 1982.

Wise Old Sign Painter

Talked to an old sign painter
I passed on the road the other day.
One of the more interesting folk you could meet,
With those worn-out shoes and brand-new brushes.
I wondered if he had traveled very far
To get those brand-new brushes,
So when I asked him how far he'd been,
He just smiled and showed me this freshly painted sign:
>   *When you begin to feel the ruts,*
>   *It's time to change your path.*

I smiled as I read his sign, and looked back
At his shoes and the brushes and his smile.

> Nov., 1982.

THOUGHTS/Britt Boswell

To Those Who Wait

Peace may yet come
To those who wait.
But what of that
Peace and when, oh
When shall it come?
If only after a wait,
Then why not now,
When the people
Call out so...
Call out for Peace
Now, they cannot wait.

              Nov., 1982.

The Taoist on nuclear proliferation
as it is written in Tao Te Ching:
    "He who knows when to stop does
    not find himself in trouble.
    He will stay forever safe."
The time to stop nuclear proliferation
is now, in order to stay forever safe.

A Voice That Must Be Heard

Outside, the shouting echoes down the streets.
Inside, the noise of the evening news blankets the room.
Upstairs, the collective voice of children playing;
The children's voice, the voice among voices,
The voice that must be heard above all others,
The voice of Peace.

              Nov., 1982.

THOUGHTS/Britt Boswell

A Child With A Smile

Expressing joy in the simplest of experiences,
  The sight of ducks, feeding, for the first time;
  The sight of pups, playing, for the first time;
  The sight of a ball, rolling, for the first time;
Brings a smile that springs across the face,
  A smile that comes when innocence meets experience;
  A smile that expresses joy at each 'first time';
  A smile that is a child's, but not just a child's.

Nov., 1982.

" . . .your eyes make a circle,
I see you when I go in there."

Bono Vox.

THOUGHTS/Britt Boswell

Beyond The Bright TV Screen Light

*Staring silently at the bright TV Screen light,
Bombarded with commercial video every fifteen minutes;*

*Do I need this new car, this light beer, these tight jeans?
Can I live without more of this material stuff?*

Then I remember that the revolution will not be televised.

Nov., 1982, with an acknowledgement to Gil Scott-Heron.

The Revolution . . . when "Search For Tommorrow," "The Beverly Hillbillies," and "Hooterville Junction" will no longer be so damn relevant. Gil Scott-Heron.

Be Witty In The White House
or: an anecdote a day will
keep the voters at bay. . .

*Remember to be witty
On your way to the White House.
Know that leadership simply means
Having the courage to blame your
Country's ills on those who came before you.*

. . .those who were simply not witty.

     Nov., 1982
     for my president
     Ronald Wilson Regan.

THOUGHTS/Britt Boswell

James Watt's Pac-Man At The Grand Canyon
    (its "use value" finally realized)

"It's such a beautiful sight"
    he was heard to say
With the brilliant colors that seem to flash
    before your eyes
As you maneuver around from
    corner to corner.

Scoring more points
    at every turn
"It's such a beautiful sight"
    the Pac-Man
And he's so glad that it's finally
    made the canyon.

                        Dec., 1982.

. . .Forgive them all,
for they know not
what they do. . .
but make 'em stop.

THOUGHTS/Britt Boswell

That Winter Day

The early morning sun
Brightened the frozen fields
So clearly and crisply,
That it was impossible
Not to truly awaken,
And tingle with the warmth
That simply living had given.

    Dec., 1982.

Where It Really Matters

Take me to the mountains,
Take me to the oceans,
Take me to the forests.
Just take me away from the TV daze,
And back to the natural life,
Where it really matters.

    Dec., 1982.

THOUGHTS/Britt Boswell

A Vision, With Eyes Closed

With eyes closed just now, what do you see?
. . .red, with white lines running, around.
You see the reflection of your tired eyes,
. . .you have been awake too long!

With eyes still closed, what do you see?
. . .green trees, surrounding a beautiful face.
You are dreaming now,
. . .don't wake up, you have a vision!

With eyes closed tightly, what do you see?
. . .blackness, totally surrounding blackness.
You are sleeping, wake up,
. . .you have been asleep too long!

                                         Dec., 1982.

Got The Picture?

I think I've got the picture now,
It's hanging, there, on the wall.
It's hung a little crooked, maybe;
But nailed, no way it will fall.

                                           Dec., 1982.

THOUGHTS/Britt Boswell

The Coming, Soon

Lost in my beginningless dream,
I know She's coming, soon.
My salvation from the darkened room, dimly lit.

To take me away from this TV life,
To renew my senses, to rest my eyes,
To lift my spirits, to stop my lies.

I know She's coming, soon,
And I'll awaken from
This sleepless sleep.

                    Dec., 1982.

Only An Afternoon Sleep

Reminded of the sleep, interrupted, with the early morning rise,
And feeling the drowsiness of a rainy afternoon,
Sleep comes as the late day's light fades away.

Awakened abruptly in the night-time's darkness,
And facing the confinement that a brick wall brings,
A moment of fear shakes throughout, before the realization.

That it was only an afternoon sleep.

                    Dec., 1982.

THOUGHTS/Britt Boswell

Just Imagine

Just imagine
Believing everything
Everyone ever told you
And living your life
On broken and kept promises
Being happy and disappointed
And not knowing the difference
Then suddenly being told
That it was all a lie, everything.

You wouldn't believe it would you?

Dec., 1982.

Note: Gardening seems an appealing hobby within the context of a parking lot existence.

THOUGHTS/Britt Boswell

Life, Paradoxically Speaking

Life, which is to be loved
    for all that it is,
    and all that it is not.
Life, whose range of paradox
    becomes too great
    only if the door is closed,
    and the lights are turned out.

              Dec., 1982.

B.P. At H.C., Ideologically Speaking
  (Before Prep, at Hendrix College)

Those days when we would sit
And watch the freshman class
Walk through the scattered pecan shells
From high atop the underground library;

Those days when you could see beautiful people
For what they were, people with beautiful differences,
Especially when they would be walking barefoot;
Oh, for some beautiful bare feet!

Like the ones you would see B.P.,
Before Prep, ideologically speaking.

              Dec., 1982.

THOUGHTS/Britt Boswell

A Note, Simply Scribbled

In a darkened, smoky room,
People gathered to talk and listen,
All the while looking and longing;
Caught up in quiet conversation,
I hardly noticed the piece of paper
Passing under my outstretched arm;
"Am I wrong? Am I right? Can't help myself!," simply scribbled.
I turned, slowly, so as not to be disruptive
To the continuing conversation in my dark corner;
I saw the long, lightly brown hair
And caught the glance between the curls,
And wondered if there was more to that message
Than met my tired, empty eyes.

That message became clear all too soon;
Gripped by loneliness in a darkened, smoky room,
Was she wrong? Was she right? Where is she now?
. . .can't help myself.

                                        Dec., 1982.

THOUGHTS/Britt Boswell

When Our Spirits Raced

Remember the time
We shared some thoughts
And our spirits raced,
To one another...

The embrace we made
Was so warm and full,
That we forgot the miles
And just loved.

    Jan., 1983.

Living, With The Beat

When you have the beat,
And you step right out,
And move in time,
And throw your head back,
And laugh out loud,
Then lean back...
And smile.

    Jan., 1983.

THOUGHTS/Britt Boswell

Maya Angelou
Woman
Is Power
Is The Human Spirit,
Liberated
Power
That Moves

Power That Is Still Moving.

    Jan., 1983.
   After the experience
   of Maya Angelou;
   at Hendrix College.

"I've got many rivers to cross, and it's only my will, that keeps me alive..."

          Jimmy Cliff.
          "Many Rivers to Cross"

THOUGHTS/Britt Boswell

Confusion Rains

Lost in the deepening mist,
Shadows break through,
Lonely trees, rising up
From the surface of the lake;
Only to become emersed
In the thickening haze
That spreads out
With the falling rain.

           Feb., 1983.

Barnacled And Broken

Running from the beach, outward,
Timbers, barnacled and broken.
Taking a pounding
That comes, constantly,
In waves, curling and breaking.

Of the ocean:
Giving life, breaking timbers.

           Feb., 1983.

THOUGHTS/Britt Boswell

Very Much Alive

*Why Do I Sit
And Think
Of This World
Far Removed
From It
And Those Others
Who Seem
To Touch
And Laugh
And Feel. . .*

*After All,
We Are,
One And All,
Very Much Alive.*

        July, 1983.

THOUGHTS/Britt Boswell

The Pain (all over me)

Now that I choose to confront my fears,
You'd think that I could fight back the tears;
Yet, I strain to see beyond what's deep inside,
With the hope that I'll no longer need to confide;
Then I turn my back so that you won't see
The pain, now written, all over me.

Aug., 1983.

Adrift

Adrift, floating, far, far removed;
Yet, so involved, a selfish intensity
That will not abate; tirelessly sitting,
And staring, at blank walls, blank pages;
All the while, reeling inside,
With visions, memories . . . pictures of the past;
A face, a name, a place, rush in
To fill the empty, lonely room.

A stale existence, and so unnecessary,
But it is mine, I own it now.

June, 1984.

THOUGHTS/Britt Boswell

My Fear

I feel so heavy
With all my pain
Bearing down upon me
Not quite enough
To make me break
Only the fear

. . .of more pain.

        June, 1984.

The Shower!

Don't turn up that heat!
It'll only leave you feelin' weak!
This is no pleasure trip!
This is to get you clean!

Now, don't stay in there too long!

        July, 1984.

THOUGHTS/Britt Boswell

Nurturing Soul

She is a big hug.
She is a slice of homemade, fresh-picked, apple pie.
She is a large glass of milk, sometimes malted.
She is a big smile of encouragement.

She, is a trusting, nurturing soul,
A real teacher, a lifetime spent.
Even now, giving, giving, giving,
Sustaining life.

      July, 1984
      For my grandmother.

As my mom said,
  "Cabbage to the rabbits,
  old bread, to the birds."
. . .indeed.

      July, 1984.

"I went to the woods because I wished to live deliberately, to front only the essential facts of life, and see if I could not learn what it had to teach, and not, when I came to die, discover that I had not lived."

      Henry David Thoreau
      from "Walden."

. . .then again, there's group therapy.

THOUGHTS/Britt Boswell

The Longing

To return to time, forever lost.
To go beyond my fear, my pain.

Wasn't it a mountain climb,
    and the glory, within, and without?
Wasn't it the sleep, under the stars.
    and the awakening, with dew on my face?
Wasn't it that first-time bathe, in that clear, cold stream,
    and the exhilaration, with a shake, and a shout?

It was a climb, the stars, the dew, the stream,
Yes, all; to get clean.

Aug., 1984.

"In wildness is the preservation of the world."

Henry David Thoreau.

The Longing

THOUGHTS/Britt Boswell

More Than Words

Just Sitting
    under the cool, midnight sky
    on those cool, concrete steps;
    I touched you, you touched me,
    in a hug, warm, and full.

The Energy
    lights up within our eyes,
    explodes, deep, within our souls;
    it's not that we've been apart,
    no, it's that shared sense, unspoken.

More Than Words
    just a wish, a dream, a hope
    that the message comes through
    in our shared glance,
    then, our shared smile.

Because we've been friends
Since long before we met.

                          Aug., 1984.

THOUGHTS/Britt Boswell

The Power

We, you and I, unwrap the blanket
    around each of our souls.
As we sit there, bare, I feel
    you tremble, then I shake.
We, you and I, left there, to confront our Selves,
    to go beyond our fears.
As the tears pour from your eyes,
    I reach deep, within my well, of pain.
My tears, like rain, begin to drop,
    as my pain, like thunder, crashes down, inside me.
As our hands reach for the other's
    we touch, then clasp, then hold.
We, you and I, hold on to our moment,
    beyond our flesh, within our souls.

We, you and I, revel in the power
    in our souls, now bared; in our hands, now held.

                                            Aug., 1984.

THOUGHTS/Britt Boswell

Will We Know?

*When I express
My wonder,
My amazement,
Do you
Hear me,
Feel me?*

*When you touch
Your wonder,
Your amazement,
Will I
Hear you,
Feel you?*

*How. . .
Will we know?*

      Aug., 1984.

Determined

*One Word;
I Shall
Come Through,
Like The Flame
That Burns
Inside Me,
Never Extinguished,
Burning Brightly
Now. . .
I Am
Determined.*

      Aug., 1984.

THOUGHTS/Britt Boswell

On Being a "Bleeding Heart" liberal:
    If, by "bleeding heart," you are referring
to the description of the heart of a person
known as Jesus Christ, then, yes, I'll claim that heart.
    I'll claim that heart over any stone-cold heart
that clings, steadfastly, to ignorance, anger and
indifference in such a way so as to contribute to
those stone, cold walls that, oftentimes, separate
us all as human beings.

                                                Aug., 1984.

THOUGHTS/Britt Boswell

I Meant To Say

Maybe you didn't know,
I was so glad
I saw you, that day;
I was so down,
Deep, within my pain;
Before we parted,
We shared a hug,
(full, and good);
And, later, as I sat, at home,
Eyes closed, within my four walls,
I began to see,
So much more, clearly;
I watched us embrace, and
Everything was okay, again;
I remember I said
I liked you,
I know, (now), I was glad
I saw you, and
We shared that hug;
You see, I smiled as I wrote
These words I meant to say,
On that day.

        Sept., 1984.
        Just one day, out of so many.

THOUGHTS/Britt Boswell

Poetry

*An economy of words
expressed in such a way
that is powerful, affective
and evocative. . .*

> Sept., 1984.
> Early one morning
> after an effective sleep.

Desperate Ones

*They Follow You,
I Follow You, Too;
We Follow You,
Follow You There;
Never To Get,
No, Never To Get
Us . . . Anywhere.*

> Oct., 1984.

THOUGHTS/Britt Boswell

Can You. . . (Are You Able, Do You Know How?)

Can you see
 in the night-time's light?
Can you choose
 to either stand or fight?
Can you imagine
 what happens when someone dies?
Can you believe
 our reaction when someone cries!

                          Oct., 1984.

The Echo (we kill our prophets)

Their words still burn
Within my heart;
Their voices still ring
Within my head;

I believe I have seen them
Alive . . . again;
Sharing the dream
That might have been.

           Oct., 1984.

THOUGHTS/Britt Boswell

The Music

*I have lived
In both worlds;
The sounds
Of voices . . . (others),
Of silence . . . (solitude).*

*Only just now
Do I choose
To fill
My sounds
With the music,*

*Nourish me,
Nourish me.*

    Oct., 1984.

THOUGHTS/Britt Boswell

Silent Scream

It is my sudden fall
soon after that unreturned call;

It is my inner rage
just staring at the empty page;

It is my silent scream
upon recognizing the broken dream.

                Oct., 1984

The Relevance (Social Applicability) Of Jeans, Button-Fly

I soon began to tire
of my constant fear
that the fly of my jeans
was only half-zipped;
it was then that I decided
to take that long leap
and wear those jeans
with the button-fly.

          Oct., 1984.

THOUGHTS/Britt Boswell

The truth (Not That Which Is True)

We have learned enough now to be afraid
Of that which we know to be true;
So we choose the path of least resistence,
We seek the shelter of the repeated word;
Without question, only an answer,
To keep us safe from our knowledge.

. . .You seem all too eager to burn that book
for the warmth that its fleeting flame provides,
rather than to continue the eternal search
for knowledge within the reality that comes
with the turn of each page.

       Oct., 1984.

Search

I am lost, I am lost,
Your words cannot find me;
I am lost, I am lost,
I am deep within myself.

     Oct., 1984.

THOUGHTS/Britt Boswell

My Eyes, Your Eyes

Poised; Standing; Stoic;
Staring at my mirrored image.

Desperate; Running; Frantic;
Looking into the eyes of others.

I carry my pain inside,
Then see its reflection in others' eyes.

     Oct., 1984.

The Same Old Plan To Sell

You seem to know
The truth
All too well;

By simply reading
The words, and
Reading the words;

Over and over,
Again and again,
And then some more;

You come around,
And come around,
All too often;

I believe
I know you
All too well.

  Oct., 1984.

"...it is not enough to just read the words, you must understand the message."

    Reverend Jesse L. Jackson
    one October evening, 1984.

THOUGHTS/Britt Boswell

The New Child's Bad Dream

The thought of destruction,
That image of annihilation,
Gleaned from the screen,
Before our eyes, within our minds,
It keeps us busy, on the run,
In search of some light,
Within this darkened room.

                Oct., 1984.

Awakening Time

With fist clinched,
Thrust high,
Rising up,
I reach,
With a new sense.

I face this day
With the power,
Turning up the music,
I push myself,
Mind, body, soul, . . . outside.

                Oct., 1984.

Awakening Time

THOUGHTS/Britt Boswell

Why Not? (My Friend)

Your giving to me
Has allowed that
Which is within
To grow, to be;

I hear you now,
I take you inside,
I move to meet,
I choose to greet

My next friend. . .
Hand open, arm outstretched.

     Oct., 1984.

The Familiar

(Set-up) another nice, easy, safe, shared experience
   with a companion, a friend, a good friend;
   a warm talk, a laugh, a hug, then goodbye.

(Preface) I value our friendship so much, but. . .
   can I ask you a question?

I wonder, do you ever get curious, and want
to explore, to see, to discover, if there is
something more, something inside, unspoken,
until now . . . I wonder; do you?

     Oct., 1984.

THOUGHTS/Britt Boswell

The Wise Shopper

The wise shopper
Pushes her cart
Through the aisles, crowded
With others, hurrying
Home, where they eat
Their frozen meals (quickly thawed),
While watching their favorite
Fall TV show (cars and bars and guns).

She moves slowly
Looking into their empty eyes,
Wondering where their thoughts
Have gone; she leaves
With bread, fruit and wine,
And a smile for the checker
At the counter (courteous);
She moves on. . .

Without even a glance
At the covers of the
New face-magazines.

                        Oct., 1984.

THOUGHTS/Britt Boswell

To What Shall They Cling?

To remain blameless,
And crawl, slowly
In this journey
From the womb
(into the tomb);
Our anger builds
Inside, layer upon layer
We age, as we attempt
That unexalted escape
From our responsibility
To the next ones,
Those who will follow,
Those who cannot know
What piece of our existence
Will remain for them;

An existence onto which
They might be able to cling.

                Oct., 1984.

THOUGHTS/Britt Boswell

When Next We Wake

When next we wake,
There will be no need to take.

It shall be easy to believe;
We will have no desire to deceive.

So, in your present sleep,
Keep your faith close, down deep;

Because things are not as they seem,
We will soon realize our long-held dream.

                    Nov., 1984.

The prayer of an evicted black sharecropper (in Arkansas):

"...Break their hearts, oh God, give them tears ... make them flow God, make them flow ... until a flood comes, God. Wash away their pride, God, wash away their hate; wash away their stubborn ways."

                    Recorded by Lillian Smith, in a letter
                    to Martin Luther King, Jr.

THOUGHTS/Britt Boswell

If Two Do Battle

Two chests pound,
*   the war's sound.*

Two heads meet,
*   the drums' beat.*

Two hearts thump,
*   the guns' pump.*

Two battle cries;
*   another child dies.*

         Nov., 1984.

"Nonviolence can touch 'men' where the law cannot reach them . . .it is the method which seeks to implement the just law by appealing to the consciences of the great decent majority who through blindness, fear, pride or irrationality have allowed their consciences to sleep."

         Martin Luther King, Jr.
         (from King, a biography)

Between Brilliant Lights

I saw it,
A brilliant light
To brighten this dark night.

I saw it
Flash, fade, then fall;
Dear God! Is this all?

Until next Ye come,
I shall remain vigilant.

         Nov., 1984

THOUGHTS/Britt Boswell

Into This Well (Without Water)

This well,
Seemingly endless;
A deep hole.

I peer over,
And down into
Its hollow depths;

Without water,
No reflection,
Only an echo;

As I listen
For my shout,
Only the lonely sounds return.

     Dec., 1984.

My Butterfly Flight

I travel the road wandering
down and around the slopes
of the terraced hillside; like
the uncertain butterfly floating
downward, then up, into the air,
soon settling upon the fragile stem
of the smaller plant growing
near the narrow stream flowing
through this my enlightened landscape.

     Jan., 1985

THOUGHTS/Britt Boswell

The Smile That Comes Later

*We speak
as we greet
and talk (just words);
as we sit,
closer still;
then comes
the hug,
and goodbye;
not at all like
what comes after
the smile
(that comes later).*

*As I sit
and look outward
from inside,
through the pane
of glass
I see us;
in my moment
of silence, solitude
it may sustain,
it may transform:
the smile
that comes later.*

                Jan., 1985.

THOUGHTS/Britt Boswell

Give Me A Freedom Song

*The synchronized sounds
of the disco drum beat
up, above my room.*

*The familiar fear
grips me just now
as I look out my window.*

*Pulling out a black disc,
I let the needle lay
upon my selected sounds.*

*Comfort me, move me,
give me a freedom song . . .
it happens all the time.*

                      Jan., 1985.

THOUGHTS/Britt Boswell

        for my Friends,
sometimes I dance when I walk;
I hope You might see me, soon.